MW00329208

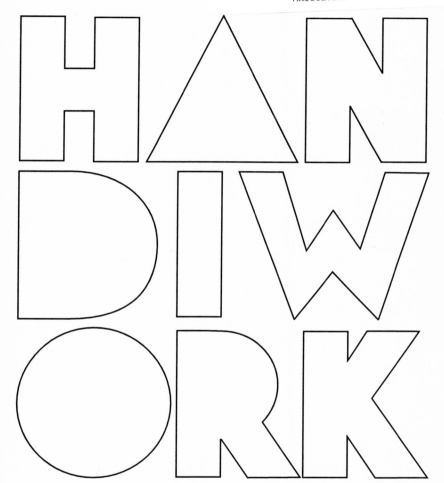

HANDIWORK

HANDIWORK

Amaranth Borsuk

Winner of the 2011
Slope Editions Book Prize

Slope Editions
New Hampshire ▪ New York ▪ Massachusetts

Library of Congress Cataloging-in-Publication Data

Borsuk, Amaranth Claire, 1980-
Handiwork / by Amaranth Borsuk.
    p. cm.
"Winner of the 2011 Slope Editions Book Prize."
ISBN 978-0-9777698-7-2 (pbk.)
1. Poetry. I. Title.
PS3602.O78H36 2012
811'.6--dc23
                                        2011052347

Design: Amaranth Borsuk and Brad Bouse.

Excerpt from "Texts for Nothing" as it appears in The Complete Short Prose 1929-
1989, copyright © 1995 by the Estate of Samuel Beckett. Used by permission of
Grove/Atlantic, Inc.

"Puttin' On The Ritz" by Irving Berlin © Copyright 1928, 1929 by Irving Berlin.
© Copyright Renewed. International copyright secured. All rights reserved. Reprint
by Permission.

Three lines from "An Upward Look" from Collected Poems by James Merrill, edited
by J. D. McClatchy and Stephen Yenser, copyright © 2001 by the Literary Estate of
James Merrill at Washington University. Used by permission.

For Rena

TABLE OF CONTENTS

Introduction   i

Salt Gematria   3

History of Myth   4

Pillar of Salt   5

□   6

A New Vessel   7

Five Simple Machines   8

□   9

Mind Like a Wine-Orchid Fed on Ice   10

□   13

The Cooper's Sleep-Work   14

The Smell of Rain on Surfaces   15

□   16

Given the Names of Places They Never Saw   17

□   19

In Which Things That Hurt Us Are Stored for Winter   20

History of Song   21

□   22

Any Taste in the White of an Egg   23

□   25

What Is Withheld   26

□   27

Blind Contour   28

□   29

Troubler of Our Sail   30

Salted with Fire   31

□   32

Both Salt Water and Fresh   33

□: A Translation   36

Paper Elegy   37

Adonics for Finia   38

□   40

Character Anatomy   41

Strasznamama   42

□   43

Mind Like a Bone-Orchid Fed on Shale   44

□   46

Lay Your Gaping Switchblade Back   47

□   48

Show of Hands   49

□   51

History of Sand   52

Answer Each One   53

□   55

Vulnerary   56

□   58

Two Rams and Goat with Torso and Sheaves of Wheat   59

■

Tonal Saw   65

■

Notes   77

Acknowledgments   78

INTRODUCTION

Brilliant in organization, cultural knowledge, and phrasing, Amaranth Borsuk's *Handiwork* begins with the poem, "Salt Gematria," which establishes the pattern of a sequence of six-line poems that thread through the major part of the manuscript. Like Sapphic fragments, this series is wonderfully lyrical in the economy and musical intensity of its language. A clue to the author's procedure lies in the mystical Jewish practice of gematria, which assigns numerical value to a letter, word, or phrase:

Rock we fill our mouths with,

  salary   by which

 we keep salt

  covenant: each offering

 seasoned, each

   season offered.

According to a note that Borsuk provides, she "took salt's value from the periodic table of elements, using the numbers 11 and 17 as constraints throughout this book." The most immediate evidence of gematria lies in the number of lines in each of the gematria-related works. In Hebrew as in English, the letter A (aleph) is associated with the number one, B (bet) with the number two, and C (gimel) with the number three. Thus the sequence ABC adds up to six. The best-known example of gematria is the Hebrew word Chai ("life"), which is composed of two letters which add up to 18, considered a lucky number. In Salt Gematria, the numerical constraint is also syllabic: 11 syllables for Na (sodium) in the first two lines and 17 for Cl (chloride) in the following four lines. Also, according to the author, "within the poems, the anagrammatic and homophonic play constitutes another kind of gematria where the equivalence is sonic rather than strictly mathematical (though in some cases the Hebrew equivalent words would in fact add up to the same number—salt and bread / melach and lechem, or king and everyone / melech and culam)." Such structures constitute "secret" formal and thematic knowledge and seem to work on both a horizontal level of literary consciousness and a vertical level of cultural, or deep, consciousness. Likewise, there are two forms of gematria, the "revealed" form found in rabbinic literature, and the "mystical" form, in large part a Kabbalistic practice. The reader, in mining this text, will discover more than one kind of gold.

For the purposes of lyric poetry, we can simplify the mysteries of gematria to their shared keeping of number, found in poetry as measure, rhythm, and emphasis, as in iambic tetrameter or trochaic trimeter, both of which appear in the poem quoted above. We also admire the lyric pressure and "inwardness" brought about by the poem's formal secret. Even the casual reader will sense that some principle is at work. The gematria poems say more by saying little. They are "pure" in the sense that salt itself is pure and also potent; a little goes a long way. In the poem above, salt is the "rock we fill our mouths with." The use of the word "salary" reminds us that salt was once so valuable that a worker's payment in salt was as salubrious as gold. Jews "keep covenant" with salt by making it an aspect of their seasonal religious observations, as in the Passover seder, when the karpas (vegetables, usually celery or parsley) are dipped in salt water.

Another central aspect of Salt Gematria is its focus on history, some of which derives from the unpublished stories of Borsuk's grandmother, Rena Berliner. In the poem "History of Myth," Borsuk writes:

> She asked me to tell her story
> > but I couldn't because I was in it:

the way a tree in a landscape
                    protects the soldier come
from digging his own grave:
                    the way a scab contains a scrape.

In "History of Song":

I often felt as if I were a nightshirt
                    full of wrens, a standing-out thing,
ready to tear the skin from my body
                    and completely reveal myself.

This is two thoughts at once. The first:
                    my mother refuses to tell me I am pretty
because she believes in my mind.

The lines of the history poems are looser limbed and related therefore
to the comparatively impure poetry of narrative, caught in time,
place, and character. This "impurity" of course is to the advantage
of the reader's understanding. The pulse of the historical and the
mystical brings into being both declared experiences and those that
remain secret, as lyric intimation. Likewise, absence and presence are
beautifully interleaved within the text, as in the "The Smell of Rain
on Surfaces," in which two sinuous columns of phrases speak across a
spine of white space. This is highly intelligent, well-crafted poetry that
also bears deep wisdom, not by bowing to a doctrine of poetics but
rather by cutting freshly into family history and cultural tradition:
"the strings that bind the sound / what wounds is easily unwound."

—Paul Hoover

"Whose voice, no one's, there is no one, there's a voice without a mouth, and somewhere a kind of hearing, something compelled to hear, and somewhere a hand, it calls that a hand, it wants to make a hand, or if not a hand something somewhere that can leave a trace, of what is made, of what is said, you can't do with less, no, that's romancing, more romancing, there is nothing but a voice murmuring a trace."

—Samuel Beckett, "Texts for Nothing"

SALT GEMATRIA

☐

My me is afraid, a little

altered   slate,

wading in.   It's going

to take me

a while to get through

all this salt.

HISTORY OF MYTH

She asked me to tell her story
                    but I couldn't because I was in it:
the way a tree in a landscape
                    protects the soldier come
from digging his own grave:
                    the way a scab contains a scrape.

These things we're saving: hinges
                    and rings by which we turn: a half
that, having, helps recall the rest:
                    unseeable space where bones are blessed,
scapula and toe: a song she knew
                    joining specimens, the way
a reader pores over a text she might
                    fall into: learning their names.

Imagine that landscape: a place
                    where landscape escapes: a hole
through which the soul seeps out.
                    Did I say soul? I meant slough.

Imagine a drain: the world
                    pours through: its waters mingle
with the stars: our oars slide
                    against both without discerning.

Imagine a longing: for one gone,
                    for a handhold to hand down.
Imagine this longing not yet known:
                    it can't be wrung: it will only get longer.

PILLAR OF SALT

[nearly nothing]

[sense before sense]

[had certainty]

[armor of bees]

Finia

[for fine machines]

[my voiced voice]

[emptied of sky]

[choiceless]

[waterhand]

what had happened

[beneath floodwall]

[watermark]

[unprepared for desert]

[who can, holds]

[a liftlight]

[a hollowing]

what has happened

□

Rock we fill our mouths with,

     salary   by which

we keep   salt

     covenant: each offering

seasoned, each

        season   offered.

A NEW VESSEL

A special commission looked into
                        my lungs, crystal chandelier
of swifts, a city, like Lwów, built
                        around a leaven, ornate organ,
pronounced me sound for study,
                        body ready as the school's
for cultivation: conservatory:
                        greenhouse with breath music starting.
Both were occupied, but my lungs only
                        pretended to the commons, encompassed
a lovely absence, a space
                        of thinking over space.
Professor S., famous baritone, deepened one.
                        Widely-admired, whiskered, one of us,
he threatened to leave when they forbade
                        my return (Father's business known)
and sang an acrid aria at the assembly.
                        The fourteen chambers of my glass house
opened, and the bears let me walk around
                        in my own body, testing its resonance.
He saw in me someone where I saw only
                        wind. He would teach me to control it.

FIVE SIMPLE MACHINES

The hand that had its work cut out for it was cut out for its work. Knuckling down on the desk, it curled to a tool not there, scissors that might replace pen with loop and lever, flexed: machinely precision—potential at rest.

The hand knew its rights, always ready to bite the dogs that fed it—stitched through with blue machismo, a need to fill emptiness. Peckish, it chiseled away at heavy matter, five limbs closed in, a flying wedge that broke down all resistance.

The hand had memories of mechanical disadvantage, times when friction with its partner kept it from its work. Saw wisdom in ignorance—increasing the distance between them allowed it to lessen the force with no discernible decrease in output energy. Pulled along the daily drill, the hand drank and dug, screwed down others' thumbs to bring new pieces up. Inclined to let matters drop, it drove the wedge deeper.

The hand learned to raise and lower expectations, forget the feeling it was always about to leap. It learned to keep secrets, accept second-class status in the world of information, embrace its dangerous calling. It tried to be self-propelled, to stay in circulation, but its calculations were off—its shuffle step tuned the dial, but after a while no music came. No soft response would be pried up.

The hand was not whole; turnabout and torque had weakened its connection to the work. The hand neglected cardinal rules, had lost its match—it had been left. More and more force necessary to achieve the same effects. But the hand was not depressed. It had simply forgotten the metal sheen that drew it to screw itself up in the first place.

□

halite,   worshipful

    evaporite   you are

colorless   crystal

        pierced   with light

your own   impurities

    turn you   white

MIND LIKE A WINE-ORCHID FED ON ICE

beautiful cousin Rosalia

    bouquet of narcissus

        [awakened]

  the things

people will try to teach you

      [ ]

          The brain is wired to destruct in case

          of breach, protect our information.

cousin

    Komsomol

      [given little leaves]

    [little watchwords]

notions could barely sustain them

      [ ]

Czechoslovakia

      [countersteps]

tell us about

    little fragments

her life and doings

[ ]

Philology: study of seepage,

transmission, transitions.

Doctor Schmidt

tall at our apartment

[calling her: wild horse feet first]

explaining

[where match]

"what we are capable of"

[ ]

Some things the hand refuses

to put to paper.

to rescue Bernard and Dunek

only to be caught

[short knot]

[in the district of belonging]

[ ]

a difficult journey

a certain hardness

a little Polish nose

[shouldergaze]

[secrecy]

the things

you would hear about God

When the hand stops taking orders,

[   ]

the brain starts talking to itself.

Prague, Poland, Germany, Paris,

[no sequence, less information]

absences of contact

not even a pillow or quilt

[unreached]

pressure preventing speech

canker that cuts roots

to shed the past

What if the hand already has?

□

Tenders of salt, shaken,

rendered empty,   still.

Harvest's jealously

guarded privilege: naming

a price

in small hard seeds.

THE COOPER'S SLEEP-WORK

Bellowed out and bodying forth, the boat
                                    set out to find its lucky keel. *Without*
          you, I have no direction, it blubbed

                    across moss-sprung waves. The inlet let its
                              breath out, shaking fungal-white
trees on both banks like sugared lungs. The boat keened

                                        for its keel: *I feel so*
          much more hollow than I used to. I fill
                              with water each half hour and have

          to bail myself out. Skimmers with telescopic
                              legs clung to its boards, filling
          the boat's front grin—face of placidity
                                        and drainage. The boat
wailed and went on, plugging its holes with mud.

THE SMELL OF RAIN ON SURFACES

Body to body, tell me   what is felt—
this self's surface,   or another's. Where
does body end?   How faceted the
between-space   where contact tells us
more than we can   compute, then less?
In arrangement   —back to front,
back to back,   hastily stacked—
the brain hates   ambiguity
and the eye is   resolute. Above all
it makes sense   of what it sees; limbs
and teeth cannot   confound it. Under
bootshine, though,   how does mind
hold slippery bodies,   how map
what's outside known   boundaries?
The brain *cannot make   it cohere.*
It's true, Dear, in this   setting
body shines no longer   —the blurred edge
of proprioception.   The key of "d" so
close to where you   "r" makes you,
dear, nearly dead.   Not knowing what
we feel makes a   handsome tactile
illusion. And if   we did so, gnosia?
Would we still   find something to grope for?

◻

Bruit of creation,

    separation: water

above and below,

    bright sea's rebellion:

an   attempt at

    rising   up

    ◻

to get closer to snow blink

    like us: into

the breach, path

    crackling with saugrenus—

river's erosion of

    crust,   creep.

GIVEN THE NAMES OF PLACES
THEY NEVER SAW

[bright, swift]

[without dissonance]

[secondhand soundbox]

skill they could not afford

at the dry goods store

[music of objects]

[aging]

[ ]

[woven from water]

smell of lavender

Sabina

[so bound in a crescendo]

her little girl

[little heroine]

every morsel for Tosca

[ ]

another occupying force

[and a small space]

we were made to share

                    [museum of kin and counting]

a small leather pouch

            she managed to hold on to

        [   ]

                    [some bought work]

and some stayed home

                        [saw the waves come]

        [Sabina opened the opening]

and stepped into the courtyard

□

Decked in nickel water,

    your nacelle: light craft

      of knuckle-borne

      hospitality:

      nef enlaced with

constellations.

IN WHICH THINGS THAT HURT US ARE STORED FOR WINTER

Take your picture? Here's your little injury
                              bread box, decorative
prison of appropriated lowerings
                              where heart swallows acorn
after acorn, each one going down
                              like an open vowel.

What's kept's ycleped cuttage:
                              panem et circenses
for us the held-to helps yell out.
                              Laid by, it points the ways.
Compass needle, sharp and
                              contraplex, what of heart's own
coruscation? All inflate. Pleasure:
                              to echo ourselves in the antechamber,

never too busy to be impressed
                              by our own function—
Wow, wow, wow, oh wow, aha—
                              doppler bubbles or rustling fabric—
this one looks cobalt, but when
                              light strikes, shines ruby!

Yes, heart, dressed so you might
                              step out, *if you're blue and you*
don't know where to go to acorn's
                              brazen buckle works. A slash
or a gasp in the backflap's
                              grip: feeling's supple
tackle, by which we are seemingly
                              caught and, later, released.

The hearts have it. Nothing lost
                              but trim and admonitions:
Catch up. Catch up. Catch up.

HISTORY OF SONG

I often felt as if I were a nightshirt
                        full of wrens, a standing-out thing,
ready to tear the skin from my body
                        and completely reveal myself.

This is two thoughts at once. The first:
                        my mother refuses to tell me I am pretty
because she believes in my mind.
                        And the second: I am allowed to continue
my lessons even though a pack of wolves
                        has been seen in the forest. I sometimes imagine
my music calls them to me, long dark sound:
                        a saw that has ground its teeth to a razor's fineness.
These are words I did not understand
                        when I learned them, a combination tone.

Yes, there is a third set of tracks
                        that crosses here: my body is present, my heart
already flown. Soon I become someone else,
                        which is just like becoming no one.

□

Old salt sailor, bad

brother,   a pinch, small ache

mauler,

chamming salt horse.

          Salacia's lachrymal

                    mach waves wash over.

ANY TASTE IN THE WHITE OF AN EGG

Tosca

        [took in the courtyard's folds]

wasn't really mama

      parted from us

    [　]

father, no matter

        [received selvage]

      [shuddered into smoke]

    [　]

then lived

      thousands

the people taken

        [a lace of steam]

           [we neglected our thread]

    [　]

hollow posts

      parents' brass bed

        [gasp we collapsed in]

sister and no matter

[cut gap]

[   ]

mother in my coat

    painted her face

      the gates

           [place of cast glass]

    one of them

   with whom I seldom talked

   [   ]

          [gave in and out]

       [hill's down]

        [lissom and gypsum]

      [pitchboard late come]

     [light through leaves]

in the street

   in a jail

there between

      [a tree and tremble]

we were terribly

       when I finally decided

□

How we know the false friend

from the true: never

eager, he hangs

    at the edge.

He brings the salt

    once the egg is eaten.

WHAT IS WITHHELD

I was entrusted with throwing bread
                    ahead of the weighlock so the boats
could skim a mealock without being
                    scenes. The one I loved had sea eyes,
made me green. When I say
                    boats, I don't mean goats, but dogs.
Each one had several shames
                    so we called them Come-you,
from the glottal, a private stutter.
                    Come-you's father gave me a letter
to toss across the sands. This was
                    long after apples disappeared
from shops. I was entrusted
                    throwing grass into moss. My favorite
thing: to eat book after book while
                    reading apples. The letter said wait
by the viburnum, which looks
                    away, then jump. His father paid.
A signist by trade, he rendered
                    the boards in local idioms
as Come-you changed. This was
                    many years before we met again
in the hearken, a marked growl—
                    before the stave and tale. When I say
hall, I don't mean all or hole: a place
                    where every empty thing is saved.
Boat, boa, bowie, buoy, beau.
                    This was before they made the dogs
dig up their bones. Sometimes it is
                    not to believe. If it wouldn't
happened to my loved ones I wouldn't
                    believe it.

□

Fatherking slew the city

and everything

in it—would not spare

even an ear

of wheat—turning earth

cruel with salt.

BLIND CONTOUR

The hand can send no messages. Cut off from its
operator,
it squirrels sensation away, trusts surface, recalls
training.
There are paths we must trace if we refuse to lift our
pen:
parable of nine dots—insoluble inside the box. Lines
bend,
hold back space, keep meaning in the dark. Each can be
twisted
and reformed, extend, lifting from the page to shake its
tail
and show its teeth.

The hand has its own phobias to exploit: undesired
touching,
short shackling, dogs. Futility music on, one almost
forgets
the isolation, regrets deprivation of food and sleep.
Estranged
from its own response, the hand doesn't know what's
happening
within the perimeter, hears animal grunts, bird-beat
breath.

The hand knows all about manipulation. Mainly, it's
pained
by the sight of its tools in less skilled arms. In the flare
between
lines: heat and hunger, waking, removal of gifts. The
line
winds us. This is how the hand discovers what it knows:
blindfolded,
up against the wall.

□

hurt in salt, gray shine

of a wicked line whip

or afterlit looted

all soot plain down

all scorn and acid

let burn

TROUBLER OF OUR SAIL

We offered him a chair
                    but he preferred to stand
with one foot on each
                    threshold. He came as he
went. His favorite sound was
                    tock. When he walked
to the train, he parted
                    the crowd with his hat.
He spat on a stone
                    for luck. He had never
seen anyone's back.

SALTED WITH FIRE

shone brightly, sun

    was gone

           [harmward]

        [without home]

         [our others]

        [paper dresses became us]

  [   ]

was a poison to be taken

      time

  [   ]

    with gold in our heels

      with his aunt until

        with him by rail

          [by thankful rustling]

  [   ]

morning in Warsaw

    time. burning.

□

Water-borne desiccant,

you draw out   the drawn

Evening levels

the uneven, keeps

its ward   a dowsing

rod   a sword.

BOTH SALT WATER AND FRESH

back of her neck

    door

        enter

Mother I

    stayed

    take us in

   [   ]

                [outside saw-worn]

was a widow

    sat down

            [home-place]

            [work of brooms]

         [small sounds make]

knitting from old wool

       old lady

   [   ]

she was

    collected from us

kept in a body

We were

       paying our monthly

           without

    [   ]

houses

       destroyed one

finally, he came

                 [those he trusted]

                     [he understood]

            [while soldiers lived among us]

    [   ]

cellar

       shelling

           [we awed]

           [to exist]

        [plural]

      out of the

       somehow

       [allowed to pass]

We were

    an and

      from where

        [city from which we began]

□: A TRANSLATION

Salt king, for what did you walk,

    for war or dreams,

everyone as

    nothing to you?

lake moon   *milk tooth,*

semaphore   *lockdown.*

PAPER ELEGY

After flurry, flight,
        I couldn't tell light
from shadow, lichtov
        from cotev, couldn't write,
recalling, air knife,
        each paper slice. Pages
returned to pulp—
        headbox a fluent
slurry of words.
        I walked sightless over
beaten and cured,
        listened for fibrillation's breaking.
Lips' numb mutiny:
        too many slip into
darkness, throats circled
        in censor's ruff, currency,
cigarettes—always surrounded,
        sundered, drowned. Mute, any
mouth hungers. Our
        books begin ground, pressed,
but never mention
        this bruised history, erased.
Nothing left save
        metonymy's numb limb:
little distance distilled.
        I can't get across.

ADONICS FOR FINIA

streets of the   city

[ ]

filled with a   dreadful

[ ]

Stadtische   Werkstatte

[ ]

surely the   safest

[ ]

Finia, my   little

[ ]

thinking and   hoping

[ ]

innocent   gentle

[ ]

possibly   hurt her

[ ]

still see the   empty

[ ]

only an   echo

[ ]

endless,   tremendous

[ ]

had to go   home and

[ ]

parents what   happened

[ ]

mama was   standing

[ ]

hundreds of   people

[ ]

Finia   among them

[ ]

thin summer   dress on

[ ]

think of you   often

[ ]

pleasures and   sorrow

[ ]

being alive.   you

□

Inside karpas, perach—

sea blossom bitter

—red halophiles, tasting

    fruit, wind,

        tears, corpus

delicti   fleur de sel.

CHARACTER ANATOMY

Few things the hand wished language could do, given up on dialect's downward spiral: words so readily betray things they're meant to represent.

Words tasted like other things. Type refused to look machined, showed the strokes that unbalanced, grew spurs against stress, each swash, spine, shoulder, tail a fresh mark of the hand that had no hand in it.

Arms broken, tissue mangled, the hand was ready to try body's cant: a disappearing text, past and future pressed into skin's plies. Grammar's ultimate loss: surface, each nanosecond, dead and reborn in microscopic fragments.

Take take take take take—that's how body ensures its own survival. The hand couldn't trust it long enough to decipher its cipher: empty vessel with hands. The body had false papers, could not be identified, clearly could not represent. It didn't look like the pictures anymore, would only sit still to be counted, so the hand learned to trust numbers—observable, firm—needed something to count on without fingers or toes now that fingers and toes were gone. Fingers and toes wouldn't cut it.

STRASZNAMAMA

They hid her horrible portrait
                in the cellar so I would not scream.

You are first your mother's then
                another man's.

We didn't discuss the disappeared.
                We had seen the wolves first-hand.

Told we could keep them off,
                stood hours in basement
wastewater sorting rags from rags—
                fingers catching cotton, linen, silk.

Later, we knit our sweaters
                into mittens
for pennies and heels we spread
                with salvaged grief: salo: smoked słonina.

One hard sugar nut each week
                to satisfy my treble stop. We lived
in the would-not of a tree—
                you couldn't see beyond the road.
Some days you read and others
                listened for a downing,
face against the out-place
                waiting, knuckles raw against the frame:
Black hat. Fox collar. Skin thin
                as a [ ]. No, her absence terrified me
most. We were born twice. We

                would never be alone.

□

Salt doll dissolved in an ocean

of sol, which

will you be, self

or water,

lechem or melach

malach memulach.

MIND LIKE A BONE-ORCHID FED ON SHALE

[A crystalline edge]

[Another entry in the book:]

[to a distance]

[a fracture of light]

[Keep me despite]

[hole the holy can't abide]

[In the blue, nothing but]

[drink]

[   ]

[About the holy]

[will make an entry:]

[come to the doorstep]

[cast leaves by hundreds]

[to plea]

[come so small]

[come severity of muses]

[Where make]

[waymarks]

[dissolution commences]

[a great likeness]

[Litheness]

[   ]

[Given just enough]

[to stitch windsmart]

[no weepsponge or quiet]

[no ledge of language]

[no struck flame]

[sail-bright]

[Bones of sand]

□

The sultan's tale: night

after night prefigures

Tesla's astral slant—

        clasping at stalks lost

to time's blast—

        stale penny taste.

LAY YOUR GAPING SWITCHBLADE BACK

The hand felt broken.
           Not to the touch, but it behaved

as if something inside had torn,
           the empty shape of pain inflicted:

innocent palm-prone
           gesture of the spent and blessed.

As though it could unlearn
           the terror grasp of moments arrested,

knowing that somewhen
           everything inside it too would stop dead.

The hand had come open,
           no longer thought of itself as he or she, instead

it lost its rage for definition,
           order, complicity, found itself unbound.

All triggers were one:
           dogshore, action, catch—same sound.

Feverish, unshelled, spun
           like a spool, the hand hissed and popped—

hasty apologia, confession
           of flesh to bone—knew itself unchanged

in any outward form:
           fear, and anger, and weapons all distorted

it the same. And shame.

□

You come with all your

offerings,   your   core burn,

sodium light

    on your face:

            hopeful, heart-

    crossed, via salaria.

SHOW OF HANDS

1. a bird in the
2. a dab
3. a firm
4. a free
5. a helping
6. a swift
7. an old
8. at the   of
9. back
10. bound   and foot
11. by
12. by his own
13. by the   of
14. cap in
15. climbed   over
16. close at
17. cold   warm heart
18. first
19. from   to
20. got her   dirty
21. got his   in it
22. had forced his
23.   back
24.   down
25.   full
26.   in
27.   in glove
28.   in
29.   me down
30.   off
31.   on deck
32.   on heart
33.   on the plow
34.   out
35.   over
36.   to mouth
37.   tied
38.   up

39. hat in
40. hold
41. idle
42. in good
43. in the palm of his
44. into his own
45. lay a   on
46. lend a
47. lift   against
48. like the back of her
49. many
50. near to
51. on
52. on one
53. on the other
54. out of
55. played into their
56. sat on his
57. second
58. shook
59. sleight of
60. the upper
61. the whip
62. threw his   up
63. try one's
64. upper
65. wait on   and foot
66. washed his   of it
67. well in
68. with a warm
69. with one   tied behind her back
70. with her own fair
71. wringing their

□

The heart, the hall

    skylit cavities of glass

    forged tooth and nail from

coal-compacted buds.

All the rest

    is fire-black smoke.

HISTORY OF SAND

Palmed long enough,   one no longer
          feels the stone
but air shaped to the   gone weight of it.
          A new wound
like the old come back   stretched as a drum.
          We didn't know
what we did, no, or   seldom, didn't we?
          So emptied, so
pine, so breach. Bent   back this way,
          one might recall
where light hurt itself   on each object
          that broke its
fall. One might press   one's hot face
          to the past
like air—one might   outlast.

ANSWER EACH ONE

[a new dark]

[more than at first understood]

[looked into the spark's mouth]

[could not find]

[familiar arms]

expected the same

[and waited]

[   ]

[gathered its tools]

[shock and shame]

obtained papers

[braced for a full stop]

[   ]

she was kind

after

[wandered inside]

[a place for put-up music]

[opposite winter]

[written: return]

[   ]

[a laying-by]

[language no one spoke]

[opened its wounds]

[rough shell]

[not new, but myrtle]

ornamental

[open your lips]

[let fly your white stars]

□

Stella, Lota, Iseult,

    stalled vestals, salute

late summer's last upset

in pale pastel tassels:

    a slatch

between rains.

VULNERARY

let be the foot-tracks
      of fleas the places marked
  with their blossoms
      we tended fires
and mended buttons
      you have to let this happen

A man escaped to the forest
      while others were digging.
A man was hidden by others in hiding.

to tell it you have to let it
      as little as possible re-hurt
no distance safe no place
      memory can't tilt so stet
as we do and did details
      mixing seen and said
  we let be the dust
      on our bread we let
  the leaving leave us
      told ourselves be ready
 were touched with kindness
      were touched with typhus
made our blessings silently
      and silently dressed

Mother, isn't it wonderful?
      They're stoning a man in the market—
one who returned—an unwanted.

let be the particulars one man
      as easily another until known let be
  the letters of your name
      be simple be ashamed

let each word contain
                    its opposite, or barely
          let them wrench free

A man had a fashionable mustache.
                              A man with gray eyes
and another wife who may have perished.

let be the voluptuous sounds
                    of naphtha and loss
          let these fuels burn up
                              their miraculous light
let survivors survive, let fevers subside
                              let snow pierce
          what it covers gently
                              and gently the wet seep in

time untunes our violins let be
                    the strings that bind the sound
what wounds is easily unwound—
                              a coil of wire razor-sharp that
                    threads us
          to air—let it stay there.

□

Blessed many times,   deeply,

we   salted   our   scars,

in sheaves.   Each shed self

kashered, cured: a shared

ash ray   or swayback echo.

TWO RAMS AND GOAT WITH TORSO AND SHEAVES OF WHEAT

if a flower confesses its shame in a little book
if fire burns only windows and doors
if fruit turns to stone in your hands
if food turns to dust in your mouth
if the things of this world are more or less beautiful than
     you remembered

if a ram takes the place of the boy in the story
if the ram is loved for the strength and quivering of hindquarters
if voices call out in the wilderness the names and colors of their
     greatest sins
if color and sound and sin all burn you the same
if fire makes animals tremble in their harnesses

if shame is only a temporary position
if things around you burn to signify their presence
if you become acquainted with flavors of ash
if ash misses the spark that ignited its former body
if you once had a body, but find it changed to something more or less
     beautiful than you remembered

if the peacocks shake off their feathers
if the ram rakes you over the coals
if your lovers all smell of combustion
if you try to talk with the fire
if you cannot close the book of floral opprobrium

if your hands are separated from your body by a blast, a glance,
     or their own volition
if your hands are asked to tell everything they know
if your right hand survives each disaster knowing it's lost its left
if your wrists ache with spectral longing for their hands
if your hands are masked and beaten with branches and wild fern

if the boy's music is known to put monsters to sleep
if music hurts its instruments
if hair smokes from bow's friction and skin flakes each time it's
        beaten
if our bodies are not behaving the way we trained them
if anything veiled in black is called a monster

if colors outpace us
if stones kick up from the fields and wind licks clean the crops
if wheat threshes itself
if you won't kiss the harvest floor
if you cannot coax back the boy, the goat, or your hands

if we beat ourselves for the things we have seen and ignored
if we beat ourselves for the more or less beauty of this world
if we beat ourselves for what the left and right hand know
if we are acquainted with flavors of gilt
if we turn up the shame to a shade of animal rouge

if doors and windows are blasted open by fire
if nothing is as we remember it
if earth turns to ash in our mouths
if the hands confess their shame in a little book and we lie down
        beside them to sleep
if the world and its colors and flames go on around us.

"O heart green acre   sown with salt
by the departing   occupier

lay down your gallant   spears of wheat"

—James Merrill, "An Upward Look"

TONAL SAW

I.

tremble | fire, | A | kind of | fire
like | running | cloud

It sprang up like a plant from the ground.

II.

o | o | o | stumble | headlong toward the | precipice.
toward the | every | echo

I want to | speak | The feeling | electric
drive on to | preach | the | vital | turning

III.

The feeling is | spread | ing
anything | anything,

We can change | hooves | We should,
to | ship | or | men

to improve | o | wonder
and | help | the | beast

IV.

Explain | the name
its own definition

how the | stone | being a man,
wanted to come into | the | house

he | says | i | just try | to catch
hearts | which is easier

V.

tender | under
those | willing | facts

the word | only holds
a | turn | now.
Don't be | a | child
be | amazing

VI.

the "Man Child" | represents
Of course! | represents
to destroy

The armies of Emperor | thrust
the city | the head

this | amazing point.
It demands worship and gets it.

VII.

the beast with | two | broken | wings
was laid out | in beautiful symmetry

with | hanging gardens | to | worship
half drunk | from | straw

VIII.

He had | read the writing | the writing
the writing that was written
and | found | it | wanting

in | desperation | robe of purple
The | dream had conquered
this | young | Alexander

IX.

power | Out | little horn
plucked up | like the eye

against | the | dividing of time

the same power | for 1260 years
fantastic | I tell you | scarlet

X.

power | the | lead | to heed | to obey
o | tell | it | it is
fallen | fallen | bird

partake | eve | of | world
a | ship | of | wonder

dread

XI.

look at | his thing
his power, | his seat,

that the | earth | gave
in spite of

XII.

intricate | city
accounted | of | flames
You | are | everywhere
inside | what happens
torn apart | euphoric
as | human torches
everyone | something
a | promise | to make | this

XIII.

A | horrible thought.
to make | eve | drunk
on | books | believing
conscience | and little children
the | greatest possible
human endurance

XIV.

a | tossed | flood | seemed | offering | answer
a | heavy-laden | promise,

no more painful journeys

strange | Scripture
those who heard | were
seen no more.

Walden | a | bit | of | earth
they would | worship

XV.

change | a period | for a shock.

substitute | Sun | for | day, | incredible!

change | the day | to | a | bath

in | solemnity

actually | do | it | and | sea,

XVI.

years went by, | all about | time,
nearly every one,

The | leaders | cursed | right in the
Sun | more than | Heaven and earth,

sea, | to keep | self | love
and | worship | Walden

through the dark | tortured
force | , | time

XVII.

men changed | on | command
to | old | ship | s

how the change | instead
can be | a single passage

from | glimpse | to | response.

XVIII.

mandm | a | sweet | break
two lovers | or | tittle | s | filled.

We | receive | heaven and earth | by | it
and | happy | die | one | more | joy | forever.

mmandm | Append
keep fresh | some little | sin
for us | to | set | the world | on

XIX.

Who | make | s | life | edible
has | the same | worry | every day,

it's out of date.
that | fear of | getting late
or letting | go,

liver | heavy | in | wonder
at | all | that | promise.

XX.

O | BEAST | of | every
wildest | kindness
choose | fire | don't want

discover | the world | that broke
this dreaded | man | or | his hand
which is | and | shall be | of | stone

XXI.

"Winds" | coming | loose
and | smoke | and other
talking

when | the | seeing | between
is | reading | is waiting
to receive | them.

it's human | stupendous
Where you stand
now! | parts | of the | whole

XXII.

You may ask | sign | sign | "sign"
to get | and put

astonishing | that the | mark
The mark. | is the mark | is the "mark

plain | as a sign | we | Keep
and don't know | know better and

are held | to | it
held | very | separate

even amid | the world in | love

XXIII.

speare | a line |
hidden boundary between
world | and | written

struggle of | the | book."
the mark of | minds, | outpouring
aster | shelter | power | plan
ague | lag | even | those

the | entire world | poured
in | to view | as | they | focused
the | image

XXIV.

Oh | Thou | thou | persecuted | voice
pour out | upon the | poured out
upon the men | upon them | only | image.

Can you imagine | the shocking | thousands
saving | to | to | to | their tongues
for eternity | and | Those who | are | loved

XXV.

close to them | the shadow | turned to
sea | and | rivers also | turn

Now | comes | another out | and
Now | Now | shields | men |
from | wicked | and | wonderful works

XXVI.

the disobedient | that do | that | have | done
work | with | ovens | the sin | the sun

of men - | were "fearful | long | despised
hiding in | the wilderness
dying from | their wants
water, | thirst, | tongue

parched throats | shrieking
for | not | sun | nor the moon
instead | chosen darkness. | chosen.

XXVII.

forests and mountains | stunning | heave | and | hem

the weight | of | great | nations

Everything in nature goes haywire
like reeds in the wind.

XXVIII.

"caught up | four winds, | carried
with | What | I sincerely believe

deep longing | in | this | learning
and how | You | giving us | eve

fallen | and sun-worshipping

"Baby | Baby | "come out

He's calling you | all of
the | matter of | matter

XXIX.

power | for us | late | and | soon | getting |
Errors | our | s | For this | that | will be | coming.

What about | mind?
There is not room

seeker for | questions | this small
book | to you | will answer
prepare | to | be exposed.

XXX.

your own | little | immediately.
And | these | dear, precious | things, you

Now may | continue
you | intriguing | page

to know | your | word

NOTES

This book is dedicated to my grandmother, Rena Berliner, whose unpublished autobiographical stories illuminate it. The bracketed poems attempt to write through, and into, the gaps in this history.

The salt gematrias draw on homophonic and linguistic similarities across and within English and Hebrew. I took salt's value from the periodic table of elements, using the numbers 11 and 17 as constraints throughout this book. Pierre Laszlo's *Salt: Grain of Life* (2001, trans. Mary Beth Mader) and Mark Kurlansky's *Salt: A World History* (2002) also provided influence and inspiration.

p. 15: "Experiment Gives Illusion of That Shrinking Feeling," *New York Times*, 29 November 2005; *Cantos*, Ezra Pound; "b o d y," James Merrill.

p. 20: "Puttin' on the Ritz," Irving Berlin.

p. 25: "Hij komt met het zout als het ei op is" (trans. Laszlo).

p. 59: The title comes from a ring in the collection of the Getty Villa.

p. 65: "Tonal Saw" is an erasure in which each section cuts through the text of a single page from *National Sunday Law* (1983) by A. Jan Marcussen. The vertical lines cleave the source.

ACKNOWLEDGMENTS

My sincerest thanks to the editors of the following publications, in which versions of these poems first appeared, sometimes in different forms: *CutBank*, *The Destroyer*, *FIELD*, *Gulf Coast*, *Harp & Altar*, *The Offending Adam*, and *The Society for Curious Thought*. "Tonal Saw" was published as a chapbook by The Song Cave (2010). "Paper Elegy" is scheduled to appear in the anthology *Al-Mutanabbi Street Starts Here*, Beau Beausoleil and Deema Shehabi, Editors (PM Press: Oakland, 2012).

I would also like to thank Paul Hoover for selecting *Handiwork* for the 2011 Slope Editions Prize and for his kind and thoughtful introduction. I am lucky to have had the opportunity to work with the wonderful team at Slope: Kelin Loe, Christopher Janke, Adrienne Nunez, Kate Litterer, and Caroline Cabrera. Many thanks, as well, to Emily Brewster for her editorial eye. This manuscript would not exist in the shape it does without the attention and advice of my dear friends (and sisters) Farnoosh Fathi, Gabriela Jauregui, Genevieve Kaplan, and Kate Durbin. Heartfelt appreciation to Kevin McLellan, Carrie Bennett, Jessica Bozek, Cheryl Clark Vermeulen, Anna Ross, and Eric Rawson for their suggestions. I salute Alan Felsenthal, Ben Estes, Katherine Karlin, Adrienne Walser, and Marie Smart for their friendship and support. My grateful admiration to Susan McCabe, David St. John, Carol Muske-Dukes, Leo Braudy, Stephen Yenser, and Ilya Kaminsky. And my love and thanks to Brad, without whom I would not exist in the shape I do, and to Sherwin, Ruth, Ethan, Lavon, Amy, and Tracy. Many of these poems are for Earl.